HOPE
FOR ALL

WELCOME

Life can be tough. We all face difficulties from time to time. In this issue we meet people who have struggled against extreme odds. The victim of an acid attack. Refugees who have left homes and families in search of safety and hope. A woman who says, 'I was unable to escape feelings of rejection, shame and brokenness.' I hope you'll be encouraged as you read how their lives have been transformed.

We also look at the life of the Queen as the country and Commonwealth celebrate her Platinum Jubilee – 70 years of faith and service. Take the challenge to 'sing, serve and celebrate' with your community this summer, using the new anthem 'Rise Up & Serve' which features on page 18.

HOPE for All is a free gift from your local church. It points to the hope found by people who follow Jesus. To find out more, ask the person who gave you this magazine, your local church or visit hopeforall.org.uk.

[signature]

Catherine Butcher

Editor:
Catherine Butcher
Design:
www.s2.design
Print & Distribution:
Belmont Press
Photos:
Alamy, Istock, Shutterstock
Publisher:
Hope for Every Home,
3A Market Place, Rugby,
Warwickshire
CV21 3DU
office@hopetogether.org.uk
01788 542782

HOPE for All is published by **Hope for Every Home** in partnership with **HOPE Together.** Visit *hopeforall.org.uk* to watch videos linked to the features in the magazine.

HOPE
for Every Home

08 MAKING SENSE OF LIFE
How model Katie Piper recovered from an acid attack

12 WEAVING A HOPEFUL FUTURE
How refugees are making the journey from despair to hope

16 A PROMISE TO SERVE
The Queen's 70 years of faith and service

18 SING, SERVE & CELEBRATE
Your Platinum Jubilee party planner

21 ABUSED & ADDICTED
Trudy Makepeace describes her route to forgiveness

24 MENTAL HEALTH MATTERS
How to take steps towards greater wellbeing

27 BEN'S GIVEAWAYS
Jen Johnson talks to Ben Nelson about the joy of generosity

28 BATTING WITH AN EXTRA EDGE
What's the secret of Marnus Labuschagne's success?

31 BAG A GREAT GIFT
You could win one of 80 books

HOPE
hopetogether.org.uk
visit us online

hopeforall.org.uk
watch the featured videos

hopetogether.org.uk/shop
order more copies of this magazine and discover more resources from HOPE

christianity.org.uk
find answers to your questions about Christianity

WEARING YOUR CROSS

JUST A FASHION STATEMENT?

It's not unusual to wear a cross. For many it is simply a fashion trend, but for a few it has more to say. Fiona Graham reports

MEAT LOAF

American singer and actor **Meat Loaf** is best remembered for his song 'Bat Out of Hell', which sold an estimated 43 million copies globally, making it one of the best-selling albums of all time. Although he sometimes wore a cross, he wasn't known to be a Christian. However, while growing up, he attended church with his mother and studied the Bible, which influenced the religious themes in some of his songs. He is said to have prayed every night. He died in January 2022 from complications resulting from Covid-19.

EMMA RADUCANU

Tennis player **Emma Raducanu** MBE is almost always seen wearing a small, discreet cross, but has never explained why. In 2021, the Canadian-born professional tennis player became the first singles qualifier in the Open Era to win a Grand Slam title. Her father, Ian, is originally from Romania and her mother, Renee Zhai, is from China, two countries where Christians have been persecuted for their faith. The family moved to England from Canada when she was two years old. Emma holds both British and Canadian citizenship.

RIHANNA

Singer, actress, fashion designer, and occasional cross-wearer, **Rihanna**, is the world's wealthiest female musician, with an estimated net worth of $1.7 billion. Her accolades include nine Grammy Awards, 13 American Music Awards, 12 Billboard Music Awards, and six Guinness World Records. Aside from music, Rihanna is known for her involvement in humanitarian causes. The Clara Lionel Foundation, which she founded in honour of her grandparents, was set up to fund education, emergency preparedness and response programmes around the world.

CATHERINE, DUCHESS OF CAMBRIDGE

The Duchess of Cambridge is known to borrow the Queen's jewels for state events, but occasionally she is seen wearing a simple cross. She married Prince William in 2011; unless there are changes to UK law, when he becomes king he will also be head of the Church of England. At Christmas 2021, the Duchess hosted a carol service in London's Westminster Abbey to celebrate those who have supported their communities during the Covid pandemic. She surprised everyone by playing the piano to accompany musician Tom Walker.

ALICE COOPER

With a stage show that includes fake blood, electric chairs and pyrotechnics, **Alice Cooper** is described as 'The Godfather of Shock Rock'. An occasional cross-wearer, he told the *New York Daily News' Confidential*, 'My wife and I are both Christian. There's nothing in Christianity that says I can't be a rock star. People have a very warped view of Christianity. They think we never do wrong, we're praying all day and we're right wing. It has nothing to do with that. It has to do with a one-on-one relationship with Jesus Christ.'

PUFF DIDDY

American rapper, songwriter and entrepreneur **Puff Diddy** founded his own record label, Bad Boy Records in 1993. Alongside his musical success he has won fashion awards for his own clothing line. His charity work includes support for inner city youth, and helping students in debt. He was raised a Catholic and was an altar server as a boy, but has been criticised for supporting anti-Semitic comments.

DAVID BOWIE

English singer-songwriter and actor **David Bowie** is regarded as one of the most influential musicians of the 20th century. He remained musically active until his death in 2016, two days after his 69th birthday and the release of his final album, 'Blackstar'. Although he was occasionally photographed wearing a cross, his will stipulated that he be cremated and his ashes scattered in Bali 'in accordance with the Buddhist rituals'. In 1993 he said he had an 'undying' belief in the 'unquestionable' existence of God but he rejected organised religion.

MADONNA

The political, sexual and religious themes in **Madonna's** songs have generated both controversy and critical acclaim. Her Catholic background is seen in her fashion use of the rosary and in her songs. Madonna was confirmed in the Catholic Church in 1966 and since 2011 is said to have attended the Opus Dei Center, a Catholic institution that encourages spirituality through everyday life. In an interview in 2016 she said: 'I always feel some kind of inexplicable connection with Catholicism. It kind of shows up in all of my work, as you may have noticed.'

WHAT DOES THE CROSS SYMBOLISE?

The current Archbishop of Canterbury, **Justin Welby**, wears a Cross of Nails, which has special significance as a symbol of hope and friendship.

JUSTIN WELBY

In 1940 much of the city of Coventry was destroyed by German bombs. The medieval cathedral was left in ruins, but two burnt roof beams had fallen in the shape of a cross. They were bound together and placed where the altar had been. Also, three medieval roof nails were formed into a cross, which became the original Cross of Nails.

'Father Forgive,' words Jesus said from the cross, were written on the wall of the ruined cathedral and the cathedral staff made a commitment to strive for forgiveness and reconciliation with those responsible. After the Second World War ended, a Cross of Nails was presented to St Nikolai Church, Kiel, Germany, as a symbol of peace between former enemies. The Cross continues to remind people of the peace and reconciliation Jesus achieved between God and humanity, when he died and rose from the dead.

The former Archbishop of York, **John Sentamu**, wears a colourfully painted cross. Like Christians around the world, he links the symbol of the cross with the death and resurrection of Jesus, the founder of Christianity.

JOHN SENTAMU

This remarkable event took place in Jerusalem about 2,000 year ago. Eyewitness accounts are included in four books known as gospels, which are part of the Christian Bible.

'The cross is a symbol used by Christians to remind them of hope,' Sentamu has said. 'It is the hope of light overcoming darkness, life victorious over death and good triumphing over evil.'

The hope he refers to stems from the fact that, although Jesus died on the cross and was buried, three days later his grave was empty. His followers saw him and ate meals with him. He was not a ghost. Jesus then appeared to more than 500 people over six weeks, before he returned to his Father in heaven. He told his followers that anyone who believes in him will also have eternal life. These events are the focus of Easter celebrations worldwide and this promise of eternal life has given hope to millions of people of every nationality through 2,000 years of history.

GOD GETS INVOLVED **IN OUR LIVES**

'The cross is what it means for God to have become human, and have chosen to work with his creatures. It means...there is nothing in our human experience that is too terrible, too dark, too painful for God.'

'The cross tells us that God is intimately involved in our lives and suffers with us. It tells us that God chooses to change things the slow way – by getting involved with us, working with us and walking alongside us.'

This is an extract from a BBC broadcast by the Archbishop of Canterbury, Justin Welby. Read the whole of the talk here.

HOPE
FOR ALL

LIFE-CHANGING

KATIE PIPER

FLOURISHING AFTER AN ACID ATTACK

MENTAL HEALTH MATTERS

A LESSON FROM SIMONE BILES

CROSS WEARING

EMMA RADUCANU

MAKING A STATEMENT?

SING AND CELEBRATE

YOUR PLATINUM JUBILEE PARTY PLANNER

BATTING WITH AN EXTRA EDGE

MEET MARNUS LABUSCHAGNE

Jesus is Alive!

This Easter, experience the amazing story of God's plan to save his people. *Guardians of Ancora*, developed by Scripture Union, is a free-to-download game that brings the stories of the Bible to life.

Experience the joy of knowing Jesus is alive and celebrate God's gift to all. Bring the story of the resurrection to life in the heart of a child this Easter. Download *Guardians of Ancora* for free and live the incredible adventures of Easter.

Download and play
Guardians of Ancora FOR FREE

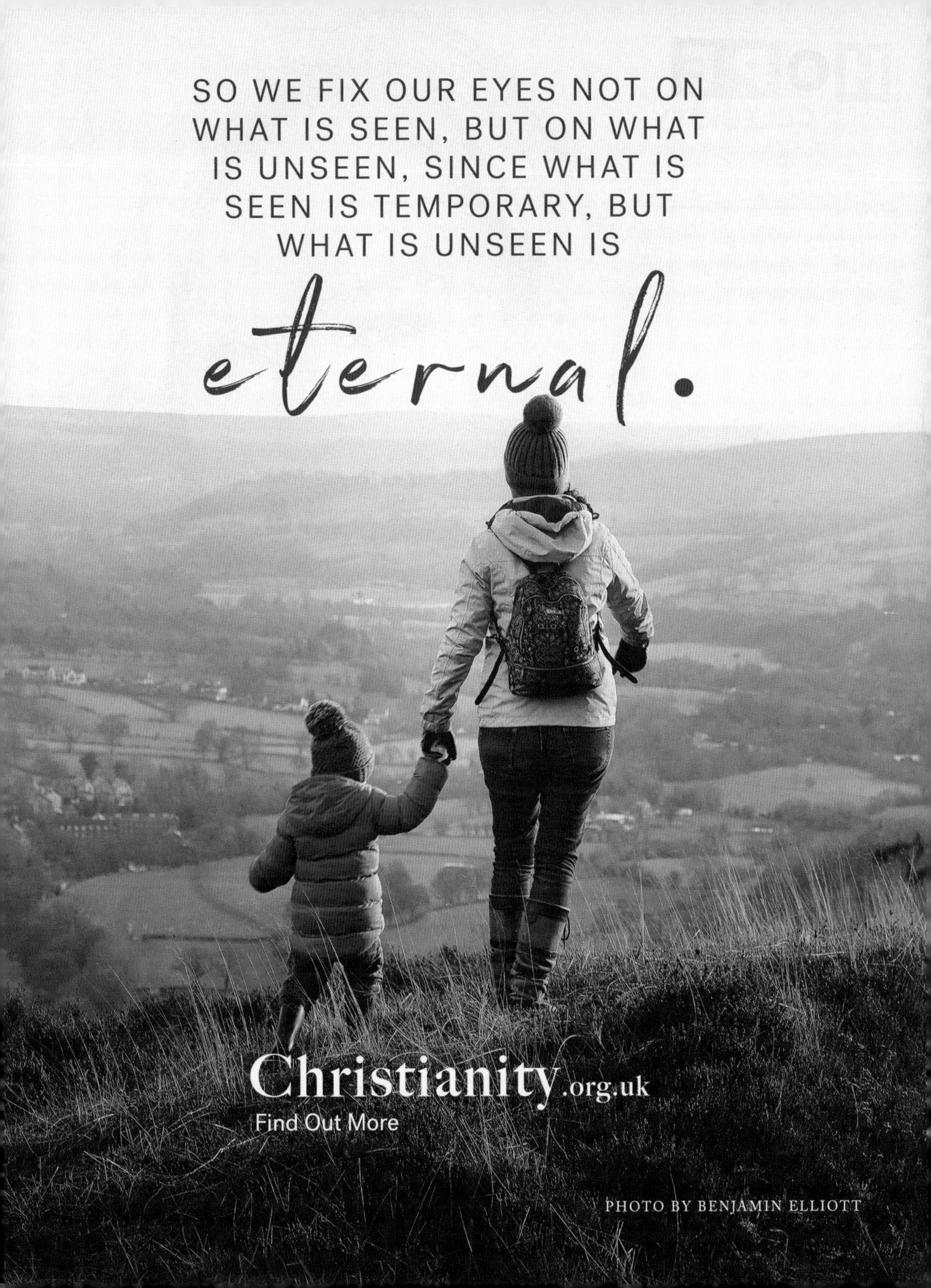

SO WE FIX OUR EYES NOT ON WHAT IS SEEN, BUT ON WHAT IS UNSEEN, SINCE WHAT IS SEEN IS TEMPORARY, BUT WHAT IS UNSEEN IS
eternal.
Christianity.org.uk
Find Out More
PHOTO BY BENJAMIN ELLIOTT

How model **Katie Piper** recovered from a life-changing acid attack. Jen Johnson reports

MAKING SENSE OF
LIFE

n 2008, Katie Piper was a 24-year-old at the beginning of a promising career. Having originally trained as a beautician, her modelling work had seen her feature in several national newspapers, and she was a presenter on a television shopping channel. But when her ex-boyfriend arranged for a man to throw sulphuric acid in her face in the middle of a London street, her life changed forever.

In an interview with ITV's *Loose Women*, Katie's mum recalled the horrendous first few hours after the incident. When they got to the hospital to see her, having only been told, 'Your daughter has been in a chemical attack,' her family went into a state of shock.

> **Katie's entire face had been burned and the acid caused blindness in one eye, as well as serious damage to her neck**

Katie was unconscious, in a medically-induced coma. 'It was a living nightmare – like being in a film,' said her mum. Katie's entire face had been burned and the acid caused blindness in one eye, as well as serious damage to her neck and oesophagus. Her skin was completely removed and replaced with a skin substitute and grafts. For months, she had to wear a plastic face mask for 23 hours a day to maintain the moisture in her skin, and she has since undergone over 100 operations.

In the early days after the attack, Katie didn't want to keep living. But, in a display of incredible strength, she has overcome this horrific experience – and has gone on to make a huge difference in the lives of many people.

Charity work

She chose to waive her right to anonymity to share her story with the world. By the end of 2009, she had established The Katie Piper Foundation. The charity aims to give physical and mental support to survivors of burns and people with scars from traumatic incidents. At Christmas that year, she read the *Alternative Christmas Message* on Channel 4. She then bravely shared her story in Channel 4's BAFTA nominated documentary, *Katie: My Beautiful Face*, which has been shown in 15 countries. She has gone on to work as a much-loved presenter for ITV's *Loose Women* and hosts the acclaimed *Katie Piper's Extraordinary People* podcast. Katie also featured as a contestant on *Strictly Come Dancing*.

Book offers comfort

Katie's work with victims of burns and other disfigurement injuries led to her being made an OBE. She also recently released a book called *A Little Bit of Faith: Hopeful affirmations for every day of the year*, which shows how her Christian faith has brought greater confidence and meaning to her life. Born out of Katie's positive experience of sharing inspirational thoughts and quotes on social media during the Covid-19 lockdowns, her book aims to offer comfort and encouragement.

Katie (centre) alongside other charity supporters who raised money for The Katie Piper Foundation

Knowing that God has a plan for me has helped me to make sense of my life

Katie says in the introduction, 'As you read through these pages, you will notice that there's also an element of faith woven through the book. I'm not from a religious family but I became a believer in my twenties and I wrote about this journey in my first autobiography, *Beautiful*. Knowing that God has a plan for me has helped me to make sense of my life. I've been able to trust in him and it's allowed me to live a free life where fear doesn't hold me back.'

Although she didn't grow up in a church-going family, it was while Katie was recovering in hospital that she first connected with the Christian faith. One of the nurses who cared for her chatted to her about the power of prayer and they developed a bond. Katie even went to visit the nurse's church when she was allowed out of hospital. But she also had a profound spiritual encounter in her hospital room, which changed the direction of her life. She shared this story in an interview on the BBC programme *Songs of Praise*, which she later joined as a presenter:

'I had come round from the coma – anyone that's been in a coma will know you don't just wake up and you're back to being normal – you're on a high dose of drugs, so there's actually a very traumatic period of hallucinations that feel real. So, after that period, when I was coherent and I knew everything that had happened... I remember thinking, "Well, this isn't just a life-changing injury, this is actually a life-limiting injury at such a young age, and I probably won't have a future in any kind of profession or personal life". And I almost started to plan an exit strategy from life.

Katie with her latest book

'In that moment, in my room, it was really bright and it was really hurting my eyes. I never saw an angel, I never saw God, and I never heard a voice out loud, but all inside me felt really warm, in a reassuring, relieving kind of way. So I did think, "Oh, am I dying?" because it was really relaxing. And then somebody, and it wasn't like male or female, it was just an inner commentary, said to me, "All of this is going to be okay, but not immediately. But please let go, please trust and surrender and go on this journey, but know the outcome will be okay and that your life will be purposeful", and I have no idea why I actually believed it and let go. I can't think why, because I never believe anything! I'm the biggest doubter and the biggest stubborn, I-know-it-all kind of person! I don't even know if I told [my mum and] dad, because I didn't want people to think I was crazy, but it was very real, and it's continued all through my life.'

Positive and optimistic

Katie began attending her local church, where she later got married to her husband, Richard. It was important to Katie that the pair attended 'marriage preparation' with an older couple from the church, because of the important role faith had come to have in her life. Katie and Richard now have two young daughters.

Katie has been, rightly, widely acclaimed for her sunny outlook and her determination to bring good out of a hugely traumatic situation. Journalist and

television personality Piers Morgan has said of her, 'Katie personifies all the traits I most admire in people: courage, resilience, determination, mental strength, a refusal to do self-pity, and a fantastically positive and optimistic view of life whatever hurdles are put in her way.'

Fuel for the fight

Undoubtedly, she is a remarkable character – strong, brave and resolute. But she is also clear about the role her faith has played in helping her make sense of her story.

In her latest book, Katie 'shares her belief that heartbreak and hardship can become fuel for your fight'.

Kamran Bedi, a celebrity life coach, wrote in his review of it that 'having faith is having hope, and hope helps us to dispel our fears and to channel our energy into what we can be hopeful for. Katie Piper is a symbol of hope who inspires us to believe that things can get better, no matter how hard we are challenged.'

Katie has devoted her life to reminding people that it is possible to overcome even the most traumatic of experiences – and to never underestimate the miraculous power of 'A Little Bit of Faith'.

> **Katie has been, rightly, widely-acclaimed for her sunny outlook**

WATCH + WIN

Turn to page 31 for a chance to get a free copy of Katie's book *A Little Bit of Faith* (SPCK, 2021) and watch Katie tell her story at hopeforall.org.uk

Spring: A time of Hope

The days are getting longer, nature is waking up. And we celebrate Easter: the promise of hope and peace

But, are you or someone you know struggling with debt? If so you, or they, are likely to be feeling afraid and depressed, not knowing where to turn.

We can help you

Community Money Advice (CMA) has 25 years' experience of helping people with debt and money worries. Our trained advisers are there to give you FREE, confidential, unconditional advice; helping you to become free from debt – finding hope for the future.

Go to: Get Help on our website communitymoneyadvice.com to find your nearest CMA debt advice service, or contact us via the link on the homepage.

Want to help others?

CMA can provide you with all the support you need to set-up a debt advice centre in your local community. If you have a heart to help people, contact Martin Bethell: enquiries@communitymoneyadvice.com for an information pack and to register for our FREE webinar **Debt Advice & Your Community** on 26th May 2022.

cma

Freedom from debt
Hope for the future

The Queen's Diamond
Jubilee Volunteering
Award 2012

How refugees are making the journey from despair to hope. **Catherine Butcher** reports

WEAVING A HOPEFUL
FUTURE

'**I** left my country by foot; it took me nine days to get to Sudan. From Sudan, I went to Egypt, which took six months. At sea, I went 12 days with no water or food. I was 15.

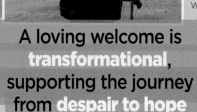

Abi in the Greek refugee camp where Love Welcomes began

'The Italian coastguard found us as the boat was not working for three days. The boys could not be patient – so they swam. A few died. The lifejackets did not save them.'

Countless refugees leave their homes, families and jobs to find safety, hope and a new life. They end up in refugee camps, often for years before they are resettled. Then they face harsh challenges to integrate into their new communities and find work.

Working together

In 2017, Abi Hewitt co-founded Love Welcomes with women in camps in Greece, to help refugees regain

A loving welcome is transformational, supporting the journey from despair to hope

their self-respect and earn a living to support themselves and their families.

The women have many different skills. One of the Love Welcomes team said, 'I did fashion design. I am good with sewing; we would sew dresses and skirts.' Another explained, 'I worked as a 2D and 3D graphic designer. I worked with computer software.'

Together they are proud to make many beautiful things – weaving, embroidery, crochet, sewing, ceramics, textiles...which often begin with upcycled materials reclaimed from the life vests and blankets worn by frightened, exhausted refugees as they wash up on European shores.

'But there's so much more to it than that.' Abi explains. 'We believe a loving welcome is transformational, supporting the journey from despair to hope. Woven into the very fabric of our welcome mats, cushions and placemats, this material becomes

Refugee women at work in the Love Welcomes micro-community workshop in London

Love Welcomes also partnered with legendary U2 guitarist The Edge who created and designed a collectors-item guitar strap. Each strap is handwoven by refugee women and includes an orange strip of upcycled life vest.

The prominent British textile artist and designer, Margo Selby, has also collaborated with the women to produce a range of designs hand sewn by a team of refugees out of strips of life vest material and upcycled blanket fabric.

World-renowned street artist, Banksy, designed the Welcome Mat

Connections

How did Love Welcomes make these connections? 'In my personal life I had never felt a sense of direction, so I did lots of different jobs working for bands and artists in the creative arena,' Abi explains. Her father, Garth Hewitt, is a Christian singer, songwriter and priest, who founded the human rights charity Amos Trust in 1985, so she comes from a background steeped in active Christian faith. It informs the Love Welcomes ethos which sees every person as equal and valued.

During 15 years in the USA, Abi worked with Becca Stevens, also a priest, who founded Thistle Farms in Nashville, Tennessee, to provide sanctuary for survivors of trafficking, violence, and addiction.

Abi and Becca visited Greece with a team from Thistle Farms and saw the hundreds of women and children who were seeking sanctuary, often arriving with little more than life jackets from the crowded boats, and blankets from relief agencies. In collaboration with women from the camps, they began Love Welcomes by transforming these items into welcome mats, table runners and other textiles.

At first Love Welcomes provided women with the opportunity to generate an income in the camps. Within a few short months, each woman earned enough for her family to begin a new life. Several have moved on and now run their own businesses in the countries where they have been resettled. Their message to the world is: 'Please tell everyone we are not lazy. We want to contribute to society.'

a part of each beautiful gift that is handcrafted by our strong team of refugee women. They are then sold around the world, with proceeds from each sale going directly to those who wove them.'

Contributions

Just as the women each contributed their skills, Abi contributed her connections, which have helped Love Welcomes make headlines and attract customers. The world-renowned street artist, Banksy, designed the Welcome Mat: handsewn mats, which have the word 'welcome' woven into them, using the bright orange material from life vests found on beaches in Greece. There is a long waiting list for these mats, which are made in batches as the materials become available.

Benita, one of the Love Welcomes team, with the guitar strap, which was designed by The Edge

In this way, Abi and the women have begun to change the perception and treatment of refugees, as their business model gives women dignity and contributes to their economic and social wellbeing. Since Love Welcomes began, more than 800 women have used their skills to make items to sell. Love Welcomes continues to work with 108 women globally, including 52 women in the camps.

Their base is now in the UK, where 18 refugees from African and Middle Eastern countries have set up the first Love Welcomes micro-community workshop in London. This social enterprise company helps women begin to stitch their lives back together. Every purchase from the online shop lovewelcomes.org creates jobs, which create resources, independence and confidence for the women. They each earn above the Living Wage and have a permanent salary, which gives much needed stability.

Community

'They all come with a longing to belong, make friends and be accepted,' Abi says. Love Welcomes provides a safe, supportive community offering training in a range of skills as well as providing access to health and legal support, mother and baby supplies, nutritious food and support for micro businesses. The team spend two-thirds of their time producing the items for sale and one-third learning marketing, conversational English and all the other skills needed to run the business.

The hope is that each woman will gain a range of skills, which will enable her to get an interview leading to a job using those skills. Without Love Welcomes' support, some refugee women had gone for nine

years or more without ever being offered a job, even though they had valuable experience in a range of careers.

Anisa from Albania said, 'My life has completely changed. I am financially independent and I feel very good because I am doing something for myself.'

Sofia from Ethiopia added, 'You don't feel like you are employed actually. You feel like you are part of a family. It's a great team.'

Benita, who is Congolese, said, 'Now I feel I can provide for myself. I was feeling quite alone in London, so now I can say I have a family.'

The Love Welcomes ethos sees every person as equal and valued

Customers

In 2020 the team asked their supporters to send messages of hope to the women in Greece. One of the messages read: 'When I opened the box with my rug in it I felt so overwhelmed. Me and my daughter stood in the kitchen and cried as we held it. It is my most prized possession. I stand on it and think of all the suffering you must have gone through, or still do, and on my hardest days I think if you can survive what you have survived, I can do what I need to do in this moment. Moment by moment we get through. And hope pushes us forward. I love you and am so grateful for you.' As another supporter said: 'You are not refugees, you are models of courage and kindness. We love you.'

For Love Welcomes, the first workshop is just the beginning, Abi says. 'We can't stop the refugee crisis that has forced millions of men, women and children to flee their homes out of fear for their lives. But we're not helpless either. We can help some of the women who arrive to weave a better future for themselves and their families – futures full of hope and purpose.'

WATCH
Watch Abi Hewitt introducing Love Welcomes at hopeforall.org.uk

Abused · Addicted · Free

When Trudy Makepeace arrived at the girls' home in Tredegar, a staff member on duty at the time wondered how she was still alive.

Trudy was skin and bone, with fear in her eyes and the staff on duty said they'd never seen someone so destroyed by drugs. This true story of Trudy's transformation is marked by the mercy and miraculous power of God.

'*Addicted Abused Free* conveys Trudy's personal story and I truly commend her for her courage and desire to share it. Yet, it is not just her story that is remarkable, but also God's story; a story that clearly expresses His heart.' – **Fiona Fallon**

'What a story! Trudy's journey shows that there is always hope, even when the odds are against you from the off. I totally endorse this book. Buy it, then fasten your seat belt!' – **Barry Woodward**

'Few autobiographies I have read have been written with such transparent honesty as this powerful book from Trudy Makepeace. I fully recommend this book.' – **John Glass**

For bulk purchases of 10 copies or more add discount code AAF25 to receive 25% off when you purchase from www.malcolmdown.co.uk

Public promises, a hidden ceremony, and a secret recipe: Catherine Butcher considers key aspects of the Queen's 70 years of faith and service

A PROMISE TO
SERVE

At the start of this Platinum Jubilee year, the Queen renewed the pledge she first made in 1947 'that my life will always be devoted to your service'.

She first made that promise on her 21st birthday when she asked for her people's support and God's help 'to make good my vow'. It is a pledge she has repeated and kept. In her first Christmas broadcast as Queen in 1952, she asked for prayer as she approached her coronation: 'Pray that God may give me wisdom and strength to carry out the solemn promises I shall be making, and that I may faithfully serve him and you, all the days of my life.'

She then made those solemn promises before 82,251 people on 2nd June 1953 in Westminster Abbey, the setting for every coronation since 1066. A further 27 million people in the UK watched the ceremony on television and 11 million listened on the radio.

Hidden ceremony

Each aspect of the ceremony was steeped in history and symbolism. She used words which descend directly from those used at the coronation of King Edgar in 973. She was crowned with St Edward's Crown, traditionally used to crown English and British monarchs at their coronations since the 13th century.

As well as the oaths and crowning, there was Holy Communion and the most hallowed moment: the anointing, when the Archbishop anointed her hands, chest and head with fragrant oil. This moment was considered so sacred, it was hidden from view under a canopy so the television cameras could not film it.

For the coronation, the anointing oil is traditionally

made to an ancient secret recipe. But the phial containing the original oil had been destroyed in a wartime bombing raid on London in May 1941, so a new supply had to be prepared.

Prayers & preparation

The anointing follows a pattern set out in the Bible around 1000 BC when Zadok, a priest, and Nathan, a prophet, anointed Solomon as king in Israel. To help the Queen prepare for this sacred moment, the Archbishop of Canterbury at the time, Geoffrey Fisher, wrote *A Little Book of Private Devotions* – short, daily meditations with Bible readings and prayers, for the Queen to use from 1 May 1953 to the day of

her coronation. Only six copies of the *Devotions* were printed; 33 daily reflections, which give us an insight into the Queen's personal prayer and preparation for her role as Sovereign.

As the *Devotions* explain, through the anointing 'a new relationship is established between God and his servants'. God's anointing sets people apart for service and makes the difference between an ordinary human life and a life empowered by God's Holy Spirit.

To emphasise the fact that she was coming to this moment as an ordinary women, the Queen's regal robes were removed, leaving her wearing a simple white dress, as the *Devotions* reminded her:

'Stripped of all royal dignity, to offer myself in my own person for his work'.

Symbolically she was coming to God like any other Christian, without any special status. She was asking God to send his Holy Spirit to enable her to take on her royal role. In her devotions, she anticipated this significant moment:

'By the anointing God makes, blesses, and consecrates me Queen: and I am till my dying day "his anointed servant".'

Anointed for service

This anointing for service is underlined by the Queen's personal faith, expressed in her duty and service to the country and Commonwealth. In 2013, when remembering Prince George's christening earlier that year, she said, 'As with all who are christened, George was baptised into a joyful faith of Christian duty and service.'

As she frequently says in her Christmas broadcasts, her Christian faith is a vital part of her life. In 2002 she said, 'I know just how much I rely on my own faith to guide me through the good times and the bad. Each day is a new beginning, I know that the only way to live my life is to try to do what is right, to take the long view, to give of my best in all that the day brings, and to put my trust in God. Like others of you who draw inspiration from your own faith, I draw strength from the message of hope in the Christian gospel.'

And, as she said at Christmas in 2014: 'For me, the life of Jesus Christ, the Prince of Peace, whose birth we celebrate today, is an inspiration and an anchor in my life.'

As her speeches show, faith, duty and service are the hallmarks of her 70 years on the throne; a record-breaking reign that's worth celebrating.

RISE UP AND SERVE

VERSE 1

In this glorious year of the Jubilee
We give thanks for Her Majesty
In honour of a faithful heart
Who chose to serve and to play her part

VERSE 2

Many nations have gathered here
From the mountain heights let the song ring clear
Celebrating the answered call
Blessed with prayer and sacred oil

CHORUS

'Rise up and serve' is the call we hear
With hope in our hearts, joining as one, making history.
Let fanfares sound through this Jubilee
Rise up and serve, thanking God for Her Majesty

VERSE 3

May God's good grace be upon her now
To complete the task and fulfil her vow.
May the trust in Christ she has held so long
Be the truth that burns brightly on.

MIDDLE SECTION

One hope, one vision
On many tongues one song
From East to West
Let's keep it burning on

One hope, one vision
On many tongues one song
From East to West
Let's keep it burning on
Keep it burning on

Rise up, come on and rise up, in this year of Jubilee
Rise up, come on and rise up, celebration time is here

The Jubilee is coming
Everyone is singing
Rise up and greet the dawn
The Jubilee is coming
Everyone is singing
Let's keep it burning on
Keep it burning on

HOPE CELEBRATION

SING, SERVE & CELEBRATE

The Platinum Jubilee gives us an opportunity to bring our communities together after two difficult years: theplatinumjubilee.com is a dedicated website with all the ideas and resources you'll need to celebrate.

- Sing the new Platinum Jubilee anthem, left, at your Platinum Jubilee celebrations – the backing tracks, music and lyrics can be downloaded free from theplatinumjubilee.com

- Involve your community in 70 Acts of Service in honour of the Queen's 70 years of service – there's a list of 70 ideas to get you started

- Invite local schools, youth groups and uniformed organisations to use the resources and lesson plans for young people 'On Her Majesty's Service'

- Download the free Street Party Planner and bring together local groups to organise local celebrations – there's a list of games to help involve everyone

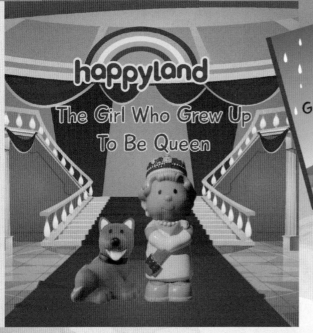

THE DIFFERENCE PRAYER CAN MAKE …

THY KINGDOM COME

'When I pray, coincidences happen and when I don't, they don't.'

These are the famous words of Archbishop William Temple. (1881 – 1944)

Having a relationship with God is the most precious gift any person could ever receive and saying a prayer can be the start. He never changes – he remains the same, today, yesterday and forever. God is so full of love towards us. He is always there for us, in every situation, in the hard times he can help you in the good times he can guide. It is such an incredible gift for everyone and all we have to do is ask, to talk to him, to pray.

Guvna B, an author and rapper recently talked to us about how God helped him after his father died:

"In 2017 I lost my dad quite suddenly and I struggled to deal with it. I was conditioned from a young age to believe a real man is one who doesn't cry and tried to bottle it up but it didn't work.

I ended up having a bit of breakdown and after crying I felt a real freedom…. It was a wake up call and realised I needed help. Where do you go from there? The first thing was praying and reading the Bible (i.e. Psalm 13).

That opened my eyes and I realised that God is big enough to deal with my real prayers, my real anger and my real doubts. That was the start of me really praying and telling God how I was truly feeling."

Pippa Baker who is now a Catholic missionary talked about the huge difference it has made to her every day life knowing that God is there for her *"my life completely changed. I have found purpose, peace, joy and courage".*

And all we have to do is to turn him, to ask him, to talk to him… Or maybe just sit in silence for a moment, reflect and maybe even read the Bible (you can get it on your phone if you don't have one) maybe start at the book of Mark in the Bible.

Phoebe Parkin, Former Youth President of Methodist Church of Great Britain / Climate Change Campaigner reflects:

" When I am in nature, I can connect more closely with God and I like to pray surrounded by nature. Whether it's going for a walk or just sitting and being within God's creation.

For me prayer is as simple as a conversation. Talking with God and listening to His response. I find the listening part quite difficult but walking through nature, being with God's creation, it is so much easier to forget the busyness of life an just be in the presence of God".

Jamie Jones-Buchanan – Former Professiona Rugby League Player & Coach says:

"I read the Bible for 20 minutes every day in silence, listening and learning in the hope of bein the best version of the person I was created to be.

Since becoming a Christian, silence has allowed me to grow, teaching me to be a better servant, husband, father and brother

Christians will turn to God for help in their daily lives including wor

Mandy, a Detective Constable in the PoliceForce told us:

"Knowing that Jesus is just a prayer away, really helps. Because of that, it does mean my prayers are 'God I really don't understand what's in front of me.'

When you're dealing with those really hard things of life and people are at their lowest, just being able to pray, there and then on the spot, everybody else doesn't need to know you'r praying, but there and then you can pray and you know that you are never alone whatever situation you go into."

Find out more at ThyKingdomCome.global

Whoever you are, whatever you do, whatever you have done God is always there for us, loves us, and wants us to follow Him. And it can all begin with a simple prayer.

As Archbishop Justin Welby says - *"The best decision anyone can ever make is to be a follower of Jesus Christ."*

Trudy Makepeace
talks to Ali Hull
about her journey
to forgiveness

ABUSED + ADDICTED

Trudy Makepeace had, by any standards, a truly miserable childhood. Starved of love, abused physically, emotionally and sexually, bullied and tormented at both home and school, it is not surprising that she grew up with all sorts of issues. To add to all these issues, her family had little money.

Date Taken

As she grew up, things got worse: 'Ongoing abuse left me feeling shameful and believing the lie that something was wrong with me, that this was happening because I must be bad on the inside. Because of these violations, wrong ideas were instilled in me regarding love, acceptance, and affection I began to shut down mentally, developing coping mechanisms to avoid facing reality, yet I was unable to escape feelings of rejection, shame and brokenness.'

And they went on being bad: 'I started to run, trying to escape the pain I felt on the inside and the challenges in the home, only I never stopped running.'

At first, it seemed nobody in authority was taking any notice. But even when they did, it didn't make things better.

'After running away, and then attempting suicide, I finally ended up in care. I saw psychologists and counsellors which only brought increased confusion and intensified my pain. I hated my life and who I was. I battled with eating disorders, hopelessness and guilt.'

> I could not fix myself. I had given up on me, the world had given up on me, and I was a hopeless mess

Looking for comfort

Inevitably, perhaps, she moved on to other sources of comfort, and these brought their own problems:

Trudy regularly speaks at events

'I found acceptance and solace in the arms of narcotics; they fed my wounded nature, and my life began to spiral out of control. Theft and fraud were a way of making money, and they became my specialty. Getting arrested and spending time in the cells became an occupational hazard. Aged 23, I began to sell my body, making good money until drugs took me to the street corners. Addiction took me to the lowest places, and I would eventually spend six years living on the streets, surfing from street to street, crack house to crack house and squat to squat.'

At last, there was a glimmer of light. 'Finally, after over 30 attempts to get clean, I came to the realisation that I was unable to change. I could not fix myself. I had given up on me, the world had given up on me, and I was a hopeless mess. Weighing only 5 and a half stone, I collapsed at a project in Bristol, on the brink of death. I was so sick, I gave in to their efforts to get me into a Christian rehabilitation home called "Victory Outreach" (VOUK) in Wales.

'Whilst I was there, I was taken to a Christian meeting and heard how God loved me, that he sent his son Jesus to die for me, to remove my sin and to give me a fresh start. You did not need to tell me I was a sinner: I knew I was a sinner. I was a liar, a thief and a manipulator and I wanted a fresh start.'

Soon after, however, she was back in prison. This time, she knew she had to turn to the only hope she had left. 'I was released with one last chance to go back to VOUK. This time I knew I was at the end of myself. After 33 failed attempts to get clean, I had

I experienced overwhelming forgiveness and peace. I never knew how restless and anxious I was until that moment

finally lost all hope that I could fix me, that I could change. When I reached that place, my heart became more open to the message and the person of Jesus.'

Coming home

Trudy knew she had to surrender to God completely. Nothing else was going to make a difference. After reading about God's love, she remembers, 'I encountered the overwhelming love and presence of God. Knowing I had found the love of a father, only it exceeded that of any earthly father, I got on my knees. This time I fully surrendered my life to Jesus and handed him all my brokenness. In that moment, he took the weight of my sin and shame.'

The impact was enormous. 'I had a clear sense of "coming home." I experienced overwhelming forgiveness and peace. I never knew how restless and anxious I was until that moment.'

Not only did she feel new on the inside, but what she wanted changed as well: 'Jesus miraculously took away my desire to use, and to this day I have never had the desire to pick up a needle or a crack pipe or any drug again. Jesus has set me free.'

The changes she experienced didn't wear off. 'My relationship with Jesus has radically changed my life. Filled with the Spirit of God, I received boldness and a love for God, a love for people, and my reason for living completely changed. God began to teach me that I was loved and how to love; causing me to see myself and others how he does.'

After doing some training, she became a Support Worker and then the manager of the Victory Outreach home, for five years. 'I was privileged to be able to bring girls from prison and the streets, and introduce them to the love and life-transforming message of hope found in Jesus.'

I learned that Jesus cares, for the hurting, the broken and the poor

Forgiveness

She was able to move on in other ways too: 'Receiving Christ and knowing his forgiveness in my own life, made it easier to forgive my parents and those who had abused me. I realised that holding onto unforgiveness meant I was holding onto the pain of the past. By forgiving them, I was not saying that what they did was ok, but I was choosing to let go of the pain that had become toxic in my own life. I want to let God be the final judge. What's more, having received God's love in such powerful way, it changed my heart towards them. I saw them differently and I knew, no matter what had happened, God loved them.'

Trudy left school with no qualifications, but, at the age of 43, she gained a degree in Applied Theology. She is now dedicated to bringing hope to other women trapped in the same sort of circumstances that she was. 'I work as an outreach and evangelism minister in a city church in Bristol, where I lived as an addict. I run a ministry called

Street Church which works with the broken and those who are in addiction to bring hope.'

What would she say to anyone reading this who is facing what looks like a hopeless situation? 'Jesus can take those hopeless situations and turn them around. I learned that Jesus cares, for the hurting, the broken and the poor, when you trust him with those areas.

He is able to work all things together for good. He will take the good, the bad and the ugly and he will turn it around for your benefit and the benefit of others. Jesus Christ is a living hope, and that means, when you open your heart to him, he brings hope into all situations and circumstances.'

Abused · Addicted · Free
The inspiring true story of
Trudy Makepeace

WIN TRUDY'S BOOK

Trudy's story is now available as a book, *Abused, Addicted, Free*, and she is delighted that the book is opening doors for her to visit more prisons. We have 10 copies of Trudy's book to give away. Find out more on page 31.

How to take active steps on a journey towards greater wellbeing

MENTAL HEALTH 2020 MATTERS

When American gymnast Simone Biles pulled out of the Olympic women's team final last summer, she was praised for prioritising 'mental wellness over all else'. Simone, who is considered one of the greatest gymnasts of all time, withdrew from the event saying: 'I have to focus on my mental health.'

'The link between a **healthy mindset** and **our overall wellbeing** can be **medically verified...**'

Dr Dave Smi

She's not the only high-profile personality to go public on mental health issues. In a conversation with Prince William, football manager Gareth Southgate discussed how he had dealt with career setbacks and the impact that they had on his mental health.

'There's very often this feeling "I'm the only one... there's nowhere to go,"' Gareth said. 'Some of the most successful people in the world have had these [mental health] issues or have problems with self-confidence. There are various issues with people's mental health that can affect how they feel or how they perform...it is acceptable to look for help.'

Many people in our society are consistently not feeling well. According to a 2018 survey from the Mental Health Foundation, 74% of UK adults had felt so stressed at some point over the previous year they felt overwhelmed or unable to cope. And that was before the Covid pandemic, which brought its own stresses.

Dave Smith, author of *The Wellbeing Journey*, says, 'The good news is that we can take active steps on a journey towards greater wellbeing. One of the keys to this is becoming more aware of how we are doing in various areas of our lives, and taking appropriate steps to see improvement.

'Let me use the analogy of a car: regularly checking the different dials on the dashboard, and acting accordingly, is vital to ensuring optimum

PHYSICAL WELLBEING

RELATIONAL WELLBEING

FINANCIAL WELLBEING

EMOTIONAL WELLBEING

VOCATIONAL WELLBEING

SPIRITUAL WELLBEING

performance on the one hand and avoiding permanent damage on the other!'

A core part of *The Wellbeing Journey* is thinking of our lives as having six different but interrelated 'tanks', each having a 'dial' on our 'dashboard'. These six key areas are: Physical, Emotional, Spiritual, Relational, Financial and Vocational. Each is vital, and all are interrelated, meaning that an increase or decrease of wellbeing in any one of those areas is likely to have an impact on one, or all, of the others.

Imagine enjoying:

- higher levels of physical energy and health.
- an increase of emotional freedom and peace.
- a heightened sense of spiritual satisfaction in the deepest part of you.
- a deeper relational connectivity and harmony with others
- the financial resources that enable you to live a life of generosity.
- a stronger sense of vocational motivation and creativity aligned with your purpose and calling.

Dave Smith says, 'My story in a nutshell is this: I grew up in a secure home, went completely off the rails in my teens, became a Christian at university and immediately began to experience a radical transformation. But, a few years ago, nearly 35 years after my first decision to follow Jesus, I began a new journey of greater wellbeing. *The Wellbeing Journey* shares some of the lessons that I have learned.'

CHANGE IS POSSIBLE!

Dr Henry Cloud says there are three predictable ways we react when things go wrong

- **Personal**: I think I'm a failure; it's all my fault.
- **Pervasive**: we go further...everything I do is a failure.
- **Permanent**: we end up thinking it will always be like this.

How can we reverse the downward spiral?
Dr Cloud recommends three things:

1. **Dispute negative thinking.** Our personal, pervasive and permanent thoughts are often false. Name them, write them down and challenge them with the truth.
2. **Get back control.** Write a list of things you can and can't control. Act on what you can control and don't take responsibility for what you can't control.
3. **Connect with others.** When in a crisis, having meaningful relationships is a vital key.

YOUR **WELLBEING JOURNEY**

This 40-page booklet is an invitation to join *The Wellbeing Journey*. Win a free copy of the booklet (see page 31) and find out more about *The Wellbeing Journey* film series at wellbeingjourney.org

WATCH

Watch the Duke of Cambridge and England manager Gareth Southgate talk about mental health in the #SoundOfSupport series at hopeforall.org

Gareth Southgate and William, Duke of Cambridge

CHEEKY PANDAS

Our Cheeky Pandas **FREE** resources seek to get children excited about Jesus, the Bible and prayer, and ultimately, help each child build a beautiful life-long relationship with Him... with some panda fun along the way!

This year's brand new, fun filled, TV series is themed on the Fruit of the Spirit, in which the pandas explore the topics of Love, Joy, Patience, Kindness and Faithfulness. This new series will be made by the makers of CBeebies 'Andy and the Band' and 'Baby Club', and each episode will include music, prayer and accompanying activity packs.

The Faithfulness episode will have a special Royal theme for the Jubilee, and will be accompanied by a **FREE** Cheeky Pandas story book, which will be made available to schools and churches to give away.

These free resources are designed to equip churches and parents in nurturing and encouraging children in their faith during Thy Kingdom Come, and will be available soon via *www.ThyKingdomCome.global.*

HERE'S SOME OF THE FEEDBACK FROM LAST YEAR:

"We need these every day please! My six-year-old daughter is going to be lost without them! She gave her life to Jesus during this TKC!"

"Having worked in schools as a teacher of the deaf, Cheeky Pandas resources might be the only Christian resource interpreted into BSL for deaf children!! But, also really useful for families with a deaf parent."

"The Cheeky Pandas are a real hit with the children. Great teaching, singing and teaching of Biblical truths. Many, many thanks for helping us as a family find an up to date and relevant resource."

THY KINGDOM COME

Jen Johnson talks to **Ben Nelson** about the joy of generosity

Ben's GIVEAWAYS

Ben Nelson has an infectious enthusiasm for life. The 21-year-old recent graduate from Lisburn in Northern Ireland is passionate about finance, sport, his Christian faith – and the joy of being generous!

Ben is passionate about finance, sport and faith

Since his grandfather first introduced him to the stock market, Ben has been excited about finance and investments – interests he's keen to pursue as a career. He was recently challenged by his mentor to make generosity a key value in all that he does.

A few years ago, Ben asked his old family friend Roy Crowne to mentor him. Roy leads an organisation called Revelation Trust, which encourages 'Gospel Entrepreneurs' – Christian leaders in church, ministry and business. Roy introduced Ben to a challenge called '40 Acts', which encouraged him to step out in little acts of generosity. Then Ben thought: 'People love getting stuff!' so he started 'Ben's Giveaways' on Instagram. Each Sunday evening, his friends would be challenged to answer different questions about life, with the chance to win a prize. Sometimes that would be baked goods handmade by Ben, or a voucher, or sometimes cash – funded by Ben's savings, part-time work, and investments.

In December 2021, Ben upped the stakes and created an Advent giveaway quiz, with 24 questions and a leaderboard, where the prize was £400 towards a holiday for two friends! Ben has had hugely positive responses to the giveaways – and says people often ask him what he gains from doing them. He is always keen to explain that he's motivated by his Christian faith. 'This is what we're called to do; we're called to be generous,' said Ben. 'If we've been blessed, and we have the opportunity to bless others – then that's what we should do!'

The giveaways are continuing this year, but Ben also has long-term dreams of changing the world through generosity. He's very interested in 'impact investing' – a sustainable, long-term poverty solution that supports entrepreneurs around the world.

'Having seen how you can bless people with something so small – I want to use that in my day-to-day life,' he said. 'I'm just a student – I don't have lots of money! But even with the small things we have, we can bless people.'

What's the secret of success for **Marnus Labuschagne**? Matt Thomas reports

BATTING WITH AN **EXTRA**

EDGE

On 17 August 2019, the crowd at Lords cricket ground witnessed one of the great battles in recent cricketing history. Australia's star batsman, Steve Smith faced a ferocious spell of fast bowling from one of England's rising stars, Jofra Archer.

Archer was at his very best, reaching speeds of 95 mph, putting Smith under serious pressure, and testing his defence. But, having battled his way through to 80, Smith was struck hard on the neck as he tried to evade a 92-mph ball from the fast bowler. Smith fell to the floor and the crowd fell silent. Staff, players, and spectators were clearly concerned for his health.

He was treated by the team doctors and returned to the field on the day but was clearly in pain and not at his best. He was eventually out for 92. The next day it was decided that he could not continue, and history was made as Marnus Labuschagne became the first player to be a concussion substitute in a Test match.

As he walked out to bat, there was immense

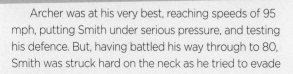

pressure. England had the advantage and Archer was at his brutal best.

Just after entering the firing line, Marnus was struck in the face by another rapid ball from Archer, saved only by the metal grill of his helmet.

The players and crowd were again concerned, but Marnus leapt back to his feet, looked straight back at the bowler, smiled, and got ready to go again. Many cricket fans would not have been familiar with Marnus at this point, but his reaction made a big impression.

That was the moment when people thought 'this kid has got something about him...' and we like it

Australian bowler Peter Siddle later commented on that incident: 'That was the moment when people thought "this kid has got something about him..." and we like it.'

Marnus went on to score 59 runs, the highest in the Australian second innings, and was selected for the third Test in Smith's absence, top-scoring in both Australian innings. His bravery and calmness under pressure being clear strengths in his game.

Rising to the top

Just three years on from making his international debut, Marnus Labuschagne has become one of the best cricketers in the world.

In December 2021, the South African-born batter, who plays internationally for Australia, climbed to the top of the international Test batting rankings, making him the number one in the world in his position. His journey to reach this achievement has been remarkable, and his faith has been key in his rise to the top of the game.

Labuschagne was born in Klerksdorp, in South Africa's North West province. His family moved to Australia in 2004 when he was ten years old and he then attended school in Brisbane, Queensland.

Marnus was passionate about playing cricket from a young age. He played junior cricket for his home state of Queensland at the under-12, under-15, under-17, and under-19 levels.

He spent the Australian winters of 2013 and 2014 playing amateur club cricket in England, in Devon and Kent, to help develop his skills further. Then, in the 2014-15 season, he made his professional debut for Queensland. Marnus continued to perform well in his early seasons as a professional and was Queensland's leading run-scorer in the 2017–18 Sheffield Shield competition, which led to his first inclusion in the Australian national squad.

International debut

In September 2018, he made his debut for Australia against Pakistan, but it did not start quite as he would have hoped. Marnus scored zero runs in his first innings and just 13 in the second. However, in the second Test against Pakistan, he took five wickets bowling and made scores of 25 and 43 with the bat, top scoring in Australia's second innings. It was an improvement on the slow start, but not enough to cement his place in the team as a regular just yet.

It was in England the following summer that Marnus' international career really took off with those dramatic circumstances at Lords. Again, Labuschagne had decided to spend the Australian winter playing abroad, this time for the county of Glamorgan. After playing well there, he was called up to Australia's squad for the 2019 Ashes series in England but perhaps had not expected to feature in the first-choice eleven to face Jofra Archer.

Following the 2019 Ashes series, Marnus' career has gone from strength to strength. He had an excellent 2019 as he ended up scoring 1104 runs in the calendar year, more than any other batter in Test cricket.

He was the only player who has crossed the 1000-run mark, and also hit three hundreds and seven fifties.

He continued this fine form throughout 2020 and 2021 as he rose to the top of the Test batting rankings in December 2021, during Australia's comprehensive Ashes series victory against England.

Quirky style

When facing the fastest bowlers where speeds can be consistently over 90 mph, batters can have less than half a second to react. The margin of error is so small that any hint of indecision can be the difference between hitting the ball to the boundary and getting out.

Marnus' quirky technique may be a little unusual at times. For example, he has become known for shouting 'NO RUN!' when defending or evading the ball. But one thing that stands out is his absolute commitment behind every shot. Whether he is attacking, defending or leaving the ball, he does so with absolute (and sometimes extravagant) conviction.

This inner confidence and resilience is vital in a sport which can be so brutal, and Marnus has spoken openly about the importance of his faith.

'It definitely puts more perspective on your life. International cricket – and let's be honest, the game of cricket – is based on failure... Most players fail more than they succeed. It's tough. And it definitely helps when you have your faith.

'Sport is a fickle game... in the big scheme of things, what you're worth, what you put your value in, isn't out there on the pitch; it's internal and in Christ... That's a massive thing for me because cricket is always going to be up and down and if you have a constant in your life, it makes life a lot easier.'

Supportive Mum

Labuschagne was brought up in a Christian household and he says he's always had a very strong relationship

He writes a reference to a favourite Bible verse on the bottom of his bat

with God. Having called himself a Christian for all his life, Marnus came to own his faith in his late teens.

His mother has been particularly supportive, leaving Bible verses around the house and even writing them in his cricket shoes. 'You look down when you're putting your shoes on and you really give glory to God because he's blessed you right at this moment.'

He also writes a reference to a favourite Bible verse on the bottom of his bat; the number 40:31 – a verse written by the prophet Isaiah: 'Those who hope in the Lord will renew their strength. They will soar on wings like eagles; they will run and not grow weary, they will walk and not be faint.'

'My wife and I and my mate came up with that,' he says. 'It was just something to give me that confidence when you're out there to know that God is with you.' Marnus met his wife, Rebekah, through his church in Brisbane when they were teenagers. They married in 2017. At the age of 27, there is still plenty of time left in Marnus Labuschagne's cricket career and we look forward to seeing what he can achieve.

HOPE GIVEAWAYS
Bag a GREAT GIFT

We have 80 books to give away. Just fill in the form below or online.
You could be a winner!

50 copies of *Your Wellbeing Journey*

'Where we are struggling, we'll find breakthrough. Where we're lost, we'll find guidance and where there's hurt, we'll see healing and restoration.' That's how TV presenter Joanna Adeyinka-Burford introduces *The Wellbeing Journey* film series. Dr Dave Smith, who devised the series, says: 'Be kind to yourself; don't try to fix everything at once. Find the one key thing that you can do that might have an impact across different areas of your life.'

10 copies of Katie Piper's book *A Little Bit of Faith*

Packed with hard-won words of wisdom and practical advice, *A Little Bit of Faith* is the companion every reader needs to grow and glow right where you are. Providing 365 bite-sized daily affirmations, Katie Piper encourages us to see that heartbreak and hardship can become fuel for our fight. This lovely daily devotional draws on Katie's own faith to show how spirituality has brought greater confidence and meaning to her life.

10 copies of Mark's Gospel

This beautifully illustrated, magazine-style book is the story of Jesus' life as told by Mark, one of Jesus' first-century followers. For anyone who wants to find out more about the founder of Christianity, it makes fascinating reading.

10 copies of Trudy Makepeace's book *Abused, Addicted, Free*

'He grabbed my throat with one hand and pushed the edge of a blade to my neck with the other.' Months later when Trudy arrived at the girls' home in Tredegar, a staff member wondered how she was still alive. This true story of transformation is marked by the mercy and miraculous power of God making Trudy a true champion of the broken, destitute, and marginalised.

RESPONSE

Enter online at **HopeforAll.org.uk** or return this form to:
HOPE for All, HOPE 8A Market Place, Rugby, Warwickshire CV21 3DU

My choice is:

☐ Katie Piper's book *A Little Bit of Faith*

☐ Trudy Makepeace's book *Abused Addicted Free*

☐ Mark's Gospel

☐ *Your Wellbeing Journey*

Closing date: **Friday 10th June 2022**

Title _____ Name _____

Address _____

_____

Postcode _____

The editor's decision is final and no correspondence will be entered into. It is our policy to ensure that your details will not be disclosed to third parties.

A BEAUTIFULLY ILLUSTRATED
GIFT BOOK TO CELEBRATE
THE QUEEN'S LIFE OF FAITH
AND SERVICE.

OUR FAITHFUL
QUEEN

70 YEARS OF FAITH & SERVICE

THIS 64-PAGE GIFT BOOK FULL OF PHOTOS
INCLUDES RARELY-SEEN PRAYERS THE
QUEEN WAS GIVEN TO PREPARE FOR HER
CORONATION. IT'S A PERFECT MEMENTO
TO MARK THIS PLATINUM JUBILEE YEAR.

ORDER YOUR COPY
HOPETOGETHER.ORG.UK/SHOP

COME AND GET INVOLVED
FIND OUT MORE AT THEPLATINUMJUBILEE.COM

PLATINUM JUBILEE
Celebration of Faith & Service